CW00693376

"THE SEASO

and
Other Works for Solo Piano

Peter Ilyitch Tchaikovsky

DOVER PUBLICATIONS, INC.

Mineola, New York

Bibliographical Note

This Dover edition, first published in 1996, is a new compilation of piano works originally published separately. G. Schirmer, Inc., New York, originally published *Album for the Young/Twenty-Four Easy Piano-Pieces/Edited and Fingered by Adolf Ruthardt*, 1904. C. F. Peters, Frankfurt, originally published *Die Jahreszeiten/Opus 37a/für Klavier zu zwei Händen/Herausgegeben von Walter Niemann*, n.d. All other pieces in the Dover edition were originally published by Edition Peters, Leipzig, in *Tschaikowsky/Ausgewählte Klavierwerke in drei Bänden/Herausgegeben von Fritz Weitzmann*, n.d.

The Dover edition adds revised and corrected contents and major headings in French and English; editorial notes for *Album for the Young* and *The Seasons*; and new English prose translations by Stanley Appelbaum of the epigraphs to *The Seasons*, based on the text printed in the score published in an authoritative Russian edition. Two German footnotes, on pp. 148 and 175, have been replaced by English translations.

As described in the editorial note, p. 112, the Dover edition restores Tchaikovsky's original sequence for the 24 pieces of *Album for the Young*. The spelling of names in a few dedications in the Peters edition have been slightly altered for consistency with modern practice.

International Standard Book Number: 0-486-29128-6

Manufactured in the United States of America
Dover Publications, Inc., 31 East 2nd Street, Mineola, N.Y. 11501

Contents

Five early pieces
 Romance (Op. 5) 1
 Valse-scherzo • *Waltz-scherzo* (Op. 7) 6
 Capriccio (Op. 8) 14
 Polka de salon (Op. 9, No. 2) 20
 Nocturne (Op. 10, No. 1) 25

Thème original et variations • *Original theme and variations*
 (Op. 19, No. 6) 29

From Twelve Pieces (Op. 40)
 No. 2. Chanson triste • *Sad song* 43
  6. Chant sans paroles • *Song without words* 45
  9. Valse • *Waltz* 48
  10. Danse russe • *Russian dance* 52

Valse sentimentale • *Sentimental waltz* (Op. 51, No. 6) 56

Doumka (Scène rustique russe) • *Dumka (Russian village scene)* (Op. 59) 61

From Eighteen Characteristic Pieces (Op. 72)
 No. 1. Impromptu 71
  2. Berceuse • *Lullaby* 78
  3. Tendres reproches • *Gentle reproaches* 82
  4. Danse caractéristique • *Characteristic dance* 86
  8. Dialogue 92
  9. Un poco di Schumann • *A bit of Schumann* 95
  12. L'espiègle • *The rascal* 98
  13. Echo rustique • *Countryside echo* 101
  15. Un poco di Chopin • *A bit of Chopin* 105
  16. Valse à cinq temps • *Waltz in five-beat time* 108

Album for the Young (*after Schumann*) (Op. 39) 111
 [*Restored to Tchaikovsky's original sequence*]
 Note 112
 No. 1. Prière de matin • *Morning prayer* 113
  2. Le matin en hiver • *Winter morning* 114
  3. Maman • *Mama* 116
  4. Le petit cavalier • *The little horseman* 117
  5. Marches des soldats de bois • *Marches of the wooden soldiers* 119

6. La nouvelle poupée • *The new doll*   120
7. La poupée malade • *The sick doll*   121
8. Enterrement de la poupée • *The doll's burial*   122
9. Valse • *Waltz*   123
10. Polka   125
11. Mazurka   126
12. Chanson russe • *Russian song*   127
13. Le paysan prélude • *The peasant plays an introduction*   128
14. Chanson populaire (*Kamarinskaya*) • *Folk Song*   129
15. Chanson italienne • *Italian song*   130
16. Mélodie antique française • *Old French melody*   131
17. Chanson allemande • *German song*   132
18. Chanson napolitaine • *Neapolitan song*   133
19. Conte de la vieille bonne • *The old maid-servant's tale*   135
20. La sorcière (*Baba-Yaga*) • *The witch*   136
21. Douce rêverie • *Sweet reverie*   138
22. Chant de l'alouette • *Song of the lark*   140
23. A l'église • *In church*   142
24. L'orgue de barbarie • *The hurdy-gurdy*   143

The Seasons (Op. 37*bis*)   145
    Note and epigraphs   146
        1. Janvier: "Au coin du feu" • *January: "By the fireside"*   148
        2. Février: "Carnaval" • *February: "Carnival"*   154
        3. Mars: "Chant de l'alouette" • *March: "Song of the lark"*   160
        4. Avril: "Perce-neige" • *April: "Snowdrop"*   162
        5. Mai: "Les nuits de mai" • *May: "May nights"* ["*White nights*"]   166
        6. Juin: "Barcarolle" • *June: "Barcarolle"*   170
        7. Juillet: "Chant du faucheur" • *July: "The reaper's song"*   174
        8. Août: "La moisson" • *August: "The harvest"*   178
        9. Septembre: "La chasse" • *September: "The hunt"*   185
        10. Octobre: "Chant d'automne" • *October: "Autumn song"*   190
        11. Novembre: "En troïka" • *November: "In the troika"*   193
        12. Decembre: "Noël" • *December: "Christmas"*   198

Romance

Op. 5 (1868)

Andante cantabile

Tempo I

4

To Alexandra Davidov

Valse-scherzo

[Waltz-scherzo]

Op. 7 (1870)

To Karl Klindworth

Capriccio

Allegro giusto

Op. 8 (1870)

15

Andante
molto espressivo

To A. Zograph

Polka de salon

Op. 9, No. 2
From *Three Pieces* (1870)

Allegro moderato

Nocturne

Op. 10, No. 1
From *Two Pieces* (1871)

Thème original et variations

[Original theme and variations]

Op. 19, No. 6
From *Six Pieces* (1873)

Variation II
L'istesso tempo

Variation III
Allegretto

Variation IV
Allegro vivace leggiero

Variation V
Andante amoroso

Variation VI
Allegro risoluto

34

Variation VII
Moderato assai

Variation VIII
Allegro

maestoso

Variation IX
Alla mazurka

Variation X

Andante non troppo, un poco rubato

37

Variation XI (Alla Schumann)
Allegro brillante

Variation XII

L'istesso tempo

Coda
Presto

41

To Modeste Tchaikovsky

Chanson triste
[Sad song]

Op. 40, No. 2
From *Twelve Pieces (of medium difficulty)* (1878)

Allegro non troppo
la melodia con molto espressione

To Modeste Tchaikovsky

Chant sans paroles

[Song without words]

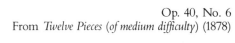

Op. 40, No. 6
From *Twelve Pieces (of medium difficulty)* (1878)

45

To Modeste Tchaikovsky

Valse

[Waltz]

Op. 40, No. 9
From *Twelve Pieces (of medium difficulty)* (1878)

Tempo di Valse

To Modeste Tchaikovsky

Danse russe

[Russian dance]

Op. 40, No. 10
From *Twelve Pieces (of medium difficulty)* (1878)

53

Allegro molto vivace

54

Valse sentimentale
[Sentimental waltz]

Op. 51, No. 6
From *Six Pieces* (1882)

Doumka
(Scène rustique russe)

[Dumka (Russian village scene)]

Op. 59 (1886)

Poco meno mosso

To Barbe Maslov

Impromptu

Op. 72, No. 1
From *Eighteen Characteristic Pieces* (1893)

Allegro moderato e giocoso

sempre staccato in la mano sinistra

Tempo I

pp

mf   mf

poco cresc.

mf

poco cresc.

sempre staccato in la mano sinistra

74

To Pierre Moskalev

Berceuse

[Lullaby]

Op. 72, No. 2
From *Eighteen Characteristic Pieces* (1893)

To Auguste Gerke

Tendres reproches
[Gentle reproaches]

Op. 72, No. 3
From *Eighteen Characteristic Pieces* (1893)

Allegro non tanto ed agitato

To Anatole Galli

Danse caractéristique
[Characteristic dance]

Op. 72, No. 4
From *Eighteen Characteristic Pieces (1893)*

martellato

ff

p

cresc.

martellato

sf

f

p

cresc.

f

cresc.

ff

mf

Pochissimo meno allegro

p

mf

p

mf

p

mf

p

mf

p

f

mf

p

mf

p

88

To Catherine Laroche

Dialogue

Op. 72, No. 8
From *Eighteen Characteristic Pieces* (1893)

Allegro moderato

94

Un poco di Schumann
[A bit of Schumann]

Op. 72, No. 9
From *Eighteen Characteristic Pieces* (1893)

To Alexandrine Svetoslavsky

L'espiègle
[*The rascal*]

From *Eighteen Characteristic Pieces* (1893)

Allegro moderato (con grazia, in modo di scherzo)

Echo rustique
[Countryside echo]

Op. 72, No. 13
From *Eighteen Characteristic Pieces* (1893)

Allegro non troppo

Un poco di Chopin

[A bit of Chopin]

Tempo di Mazurka

Op. 72, No. 15
From *Eighteen Characteristic Pieces* (1893)

To Nicolas Lenz

Valse à cinq temps
[Waltz in five-beat time]

Op. 72, No. 16
From *Eighteen Characteristic Pieces* (1893)

To Volodya Davidov

Album for the Young

(*after Schumann*)

Op. 39 (1878)

Edited and fingered by Adolf Ruthardt

This edition restores Tchaikovsky's original sequence for the 24 pieces of *Album for the Young*, numbered below.[1] Numbers in parentheses follow the published sequence first established by P. I. Jürgenson, Moscow, 1878, and continued in subsequent editions.

1.	(1)	Prière de matin	13.	(12)	Le paysan prélude
2.	(2)	Le matin en hiver	14.	(13)	Chanson populaire
3.	(4)	Maman	15.	(15)	Chanson italienne
4.	(3)	Le petit cavalier	16.	(16)	Mélodie antique française
5.	(5)	Marches des soldats de bois	17.	(17)	Chanson allemande
6.	(9)	La nouvelle poupée	18.	(18)	Chanson napolitaine
7.	(6)	La poupée malade	19.	(19)	Conte de la vieille bonne
8.	(7)	Enterrement de la poupée	20.	(20)	La sorcière
9.	(8)	Valse	21.	(21)	Douce rêverie
10.	(14)	Polka	22.	(22)	Chant de l'alouette
11.	(10)	Mazurka	23.	(24)	A l'église
12.	(11)	Chanson russe	24.	(23)	L'orgue de barbarie

In the heading to "Chanson populaire" (No. 14, p. 129), *Kamarinskaya* is the title of a traditional dance-song in Russian folk literature, probably referring to a village or region.

In the heading to "La sorcière" (No. 20, p. 136), *Baba-Yaga* refers to the ogress in Russian folklore who steals, cooks and eats her victims, usually children. A guardian of the fountains of the water of life, she lives with two or three sisters (all called Baba-Yaga) in a spinning hut [with chicken's feet] in the forest, and can ride through the air—sometimes in a mortar that she drives with a pestle—creating tempests as she goes.[2]

[1] *The New Grove Dictionary of Music and Musicians*, Macmillan Publishers Limited, London, 1980: Vol. 18.
[2] *The New Encyclopaedia Britannica*, Chicago, 1984: Micropaedia, Vol. I.

Prière de matin

[Morning prayer]

Op. 39, No. 1
From *Album for the Young* (1878)

Le matin en hiver

[Winter morning]

Op. 39, No. 2
From *Album for the Young* (1878)

Maman

[Mama]

Op. 39, No. 3
From *Album for the Young* (1878)

Le petit cavalier

[The little horseman]

Op. 39, No. 4
From *Album for the Young* (1878)

Marches des soldats de bois

[Marches of the wooden soldiers]

Op. 39, No. 5
From *Album for the Young* (1878)

La nouvelle poupée

[The new doll]

Op. 39, No. 6
From *Album for the Young* (1878)

La poupée malade

[The sick doll]

Op. 39, No. 7
From *Album for the Young* (1878)

Enterrement de la poupée

[The doll's burial]

Op. 39, No. 8
From *Album for the Young* (1878)

Valse

[Waltz]

Op. 39, No. 9
From *Album for the Young* (1878)

Polka

Op. 39, No. 10
From *Album for the Young* (1878)

Mazurka

Op. 39, No. 11
From *Album for the Young* (1878)

Tempo di Mazurka.

Chanson russe

[Russian song]

Op. 39, No. 12
From *Album for the Young* (1878)

Le paysan prélude

[The peasant plays an introduction]

Op. 39, No. 13
From *Album for the Young* (1878)

13.

Chanson populaire
(*Kamarinskaya*)
[Folk Song]

Op. 39, No. 14
From *Album for the Young* (1878)

Comodo.

14.

Chanson italienne
[Italian song]

Op. 39, No. 15
From *Album for the Young* (1878)

Mélodie antique française
[Old French melody]

Op. 39, No. 16
From *Album for the Young* (1878)

Moderato assai.

16.

Chanson allemande

[German song]

Op. 39, No. 17
From *Album for the Young* (1878)

Chanson napolitaine

[Neapolitan song]

Op. 39, No. 18
From *Album for the Young* (1878)

Conte de la vieille bonne
[The old maid-servant's tale]

Op. 39, No. 19
From *Album for the Young* (1878)

La sorcière (*Baba-Yaga*) [The witch]

Op. 39, No. 20
From *Album for the Young* (1878)

Douce rêverie

[Sweet reverie]

Op. 39, No. 21
From *Album for the Young* (1878)

139

Chant de l'alouette

[Song of the lark]

Op. 39, No. 22
From *Album for the Young* (1878)

141

A l'église

[In church]

Op. 39, No. 23

From *Album for the Young* (1878)

L'orgue de barbarie

[The hurdy-gurdy]

Op. 39, No. 24
From *Album for the Young* (1878)

The Seasons

Op. *37bis* (1875–6)

Edited by Walter Niemann

The twelve parts of *The Seasons*—commissioned by the publisher of a St. Petersburg musical journal—were composed between December 1875 and November 1876.

> "[Nicholas] Kashkin [the composer's close friend, a teacher at the Moscow Conservatoire] tells us that Tchaikovsky . . . in order not to miss sending each number at the right time . . . ordered his servant to remind him when a certain date came around each month. The man carried out his master's order, coming at the right day with the reminder: "Peter Ilich, is it not time to send to St. Petersburg?" upon which Tchaikovsky would sit down at once and write the required piece without a pause. Later the pieces were collected and republished by Jürgenson."[1]

The Seasons' opus number appears differently in different sources: as Op. 37a or 37b or, mistakenly, as Op. 37 (Op. 37 is Tchaikovsky's Piano Sonata in G). The present edition follows the practice of an authoritative Russian edition that carries the designation (in Cyrillic) "Op. 37*bis*."

The Dover edition also includes the epigraphs that traditionally preface each piece. Their English prose translations, prepared specially for this edition by Stanley Appelbaum, appear on the opposite page.

[1]Modeste Tchaikovsky, *The Life & Letters of Peter Ilich Tchaikovsky* (Rosa Newmarch, translator & editor), originally published by John Lane The Bodley Head, London, 1906.

JANUARY: "By the Fireside"

And night has cloaked in dusk
the peaceful, comfortable nook;
in the fireplace the little fire grows dim
and the candle has formed a snuff.

—Pushkin

FEBRUARY: "Carnival"

Soon the extensive feast
of busy Carnival will be in full swing.

—Vyazemsky

MARCH: "The song of the lark"

The field surges with flowers;
in the sky, waves of light eddy;
the blue expanses are filled
with the song of springtime larks.

—Maikov

APRIL: "The Snowdrop"

Pale blue, pure
flower of the snowdrop,
and, beside it, porous,
the last light snow.

The last tears
for bygone sorrow
and the first daydreams
of new happiness . . .

—Maikov

MAY: "White nights"[2]

What a night! What bliss in everything!
I thank my native northern region!
From the empire of ice, from the empire
  of blizzards and snow,
how fresh and pure your May comes flying!

—Fet

JUNE: "Barcarolle"

Let's go out to the shore, where the waves
will kiss our feet,
where the stars with mysterious melancholy
will shine above us.

—Pleshcheyev

JULY: "The reaper's song"

Itch, my shoulder;
swing, my hand!
You, puff in my face,
wind from the south!

—Kol'tsov

AUGUST: "The harvest"

Whole families of people
have begun the harvest,
mowing down the tall rye
at the root!

The sheaves are arranged
into numerous stacks;
the music of the cartwheels
is heard all night long.

—Kol'tsov

SEPTEMBER: "The hunt"

It's time, it's time! The horns resound;
huntsmen attired for the chase
mount their horses at daybreak;
the hounds tug at their leashes.

—Pushkin
Count Nulin

OCTOBER: "Autumn song"

Autumn, all of our poor garden is raining down;
the yellowed leaves are flying in the wind.

—A. Tolstoy

NOVEMBER: "In the troika"[3]

Do not look at the road with sadness,
and do not hasten to follow after the troika,
and smother the dreary anxiety
in your heart quickly and for good.

—Nekrasov

DECEMBER: "Christmas"

Once, on the evening of Twelfth Night
girls used to tell fortunes:
they would take their shoe off their foot
and throw it outside the gate.

—Zhukovsky

[2]A literal translation of the Russian (referring to the bright summer nights of northern climes); that of the French version is "May nights."

[3]The Russian word for "a set of three": applied to any Russian vehicle, often a sleigh, drawn by three horses abreast.

Janvier: "Au coin du feu"

[January: "By the fireside"]

Op. 37*bis*, No. 1
From *The Seasons* (1875–6)

★) In the original this measure is repeated once, probably by mistake.

150

Février: "Carnaval"

[February: "Carnival"]

Op. 37*bis*, No. 2
From *The Seasons* (1875–6)

155

L'istesso tempo

Mars: "Chant de l'alouette"

[March: "Song of the lark"]

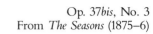

Avril: "Perce-neige"

[April: "Snowdrop"]

Op. 37*bis*, No. 4
From *The Seasons* (1875–6)

con grazia e poco meno animato

Mai: "Les nuits de mai"

[May: "May nights" ("White nights")]

Op. 37*bis*, No. 5
From *The Seasons* (1875–6)

167

Andantino

Juin: "Barcarolle"

[June: "Barcarolle"]

Op. 37*bis*, No. 6
From *The Seasons* (1875–6)

Poco più mosso

Juillet: "Chant du faucheur"

[July: "The reaper's song"]

Op. 37*bis*, No. 7
From *The Seasons* (1875–6)

*) In the original [this eighth note] is a quarter note, probably by mistake.

Août: "La moisson"

[August: "The harvest"]

Op. 37bis, No. 8
From *The Seasons* (1875–6)

Allegro vivace

8.

179

180

Septembre: "La chasse"

[September: "The hunt"]

Op. 37*bis*, No. 9
From *The Seasons* (1875–6)

Octobre: "Chant d'automne"

[October: "Autumn song"]

Op. 37*bis*, No. 10
From *The Seasons* (1875–6)

Andante doloroso e molto cantabile

10.

Novembre: "En troïka"

[November: "In the troika"]

Op. 37*bis*, No. 11
From *The Seasons* (1875–6)

Decembre: "Noël"

[December: "Christmas"]

Op. 37*bis*, No. 12
From *The Seasons* (1875–6)